Old NEWTONHILL and MUCHA

by
Brian H. Watt

The schooner *Isabella* was driven aground and wrecked on the Skateraw shore in a storm on 13 November 1888.
On the fateful day she was carrying a cargo of coal and whiting, and was under the control of a Captain Lyall.
The 23-metre vessel was registered in Banff and had been built in 1864.

ACKNOWLEDGEMENTS

The author would like to thank the following people who helped in the preparation of, and research for, this book and kindly provided photographs and information for inclusion: Shona Barclay, Norma Gordon, Alistair Hay, Mabel Knowles, George Masson, Phyllis Melrose, Carl Nelson, Norman Nicoll, Edith Stephen, Jess Wallace and Arthur Wylie. Both the photographs on page 47 are copyright of, and used with the kind permission of, Aberdeen Journals Ltd. Particular thanks must go to Stuart Christie for permission to reproduce the two poems on Skateraw and to Elaine Collie for her patience and word-processing skills.

FURTHER READING

The books listed below were used by the author during his research. None of them are available from Stenlake Publishing. Those interested in finding out more are advised to contact their local bookshop or reference library.

Statistical Accounts of Scotland for the County of Kincardine, 1793, 1843, 1988
Donald, James, *The Seatoun of Muchalls*, 1919
Hill, John Paul, *The Episcopal Chapel at Muchalls*, 1956
Milne, Colin A., *Fisherfolk to Torryfolk*, 2000
Paul, William, *Muchalls on the Kincardineshire Coast*, 1896
Watt, Archibald, *Highways and Byways around Kincardine*, 1985
Scots Magazine, February 1966, November 1968
Leopard Magazine, July 1977, May 1983, July 90, November 1993

A surprise party.

A Pic-nic at Newtonhill.

Sent in 1906, this is one of a large number of postcards designed by Scottish postcard artist and publisher Martin Anderson of Tayport, Fife, better known by the pseudonym 'Cynicus' which he adopted in 1887. Anderson (1854–1932) produced a range of similar cards to standard designs with holiday and leisure themes, which were then overprinted with the names of different towns and villages and sold locally to visitors. In this case he was attracted by the increasing numbers of 'well-to-do' visitors who were travelling to Newtonhill by train from Aberdeen as the village grew in popularity as an attractive destination for picnics and day excursions.

INTRODUCTION

The history and heritage of Newtonhill (Skateraw) and Muchalls are inextricably linked through their people, customs, religion and traditional dependency on fishing. Many of these links extend up and down the coast to other fishing settlements at Cowie, Stonehaven, Portlethen, Findon and Torry, binding the north Kincardineshire villages together.

Skateraw was undoubtedly founded on fishing, but exactly when the settlement was established is much less certain. It does not appear on maps of the area dating from 1640 or 1654, but is mentioned by John Keith, the parish minister of Dunnottar, who in his description of 'the Merns' (sic) in 1642 refers to 'many little shores for fisher boats such as Port Leviathan [Portlethen], Findon, Shore of Elsick, Sketraw, Muchalls and Cowy'.

At this time there appear to have been two distinct, local settlements that played a part in the development of modern-day Newtonhill. These were the Fishertoun of Elsick – named after the barony of that name, of which it was part – and its close neighbour Sketraw. Both of these shared the natural haven of Elsick Shore.

The Fishertoun of Elsick lay 'abuin the cove' on the cliffs to the north of the bay, beside the footpath to Downies, with Sketraw located on the Braehead on the south side of the bay. Elsick seems to predate Skateraw as the court book of the Barony of Urie refers to Elsick as 'a fishertoun' in 1636 but makes no reference to Skateraw. Further reference to both is, however, made in 1722 by Alexander Garioch, a farmer at Mergie, who in writing about the Parish of Fetteresso stated that 'it is accommodate with four fishing villages at Cowie, Muchalls, Elsick and Skateraw', adding that the fishing industry was 'prosperous enough to provide fish for thirty miles up country and a great quantity to be salted'. Thereafter the Fishertoun of Elsick appears to have fallen into decline, and by 1744 Garden's very detailed and normally accurate map of the area shows no trace of the settlement, but has Skateraw Harbour clearly marked.

The name Skateraw is generally accepted as deriving from Gaelic words meaning 'row on the rock', which likely refers to the original row of fisher cottages on the Braehead. The significance of fishing for the village grew steadily, peaking between about 1850 and 1875. In 1855 there were 50 fishermen in Skateraw with a fleet of 26 boats comprised of eleven drifters and fifteen yawls, with over 130 people employed in fishing. Cod, ling, whiting, haddock, flatfish and salmon made up the bulk of what was landed, some of it caught in nets and the rest with longlines carrying up to 800 hooks, baited with mussels. During the herring season most local fishermen sailed to Aberdeen, Fraserburgh or Peterhead, following the herring shoals. By 1881, however, fishing in Skateraw had declined significantly with only ten boats in the village employing around 70 men and boys.

The dangers posed by the treacherous coastline, reflected in numerous losses of both boats and lives, coupled with the shortcomings of the tidal harbour, combined to undermine the village as a viable fishing community. However, the real cause of the decline of Skateraw as a fishing village was the advent of steam trawlers, the first of which sailed from Aberdeen in 1882, heralding rapidly changing conditions in the fishing industry.

By 1892 there were over 30 steam trawlers using Aberdeen as their home port, and with their increased size compared to the old sailboats, their use of nets rather than lines to increase catches, and their inability to berth at the small coastal 'shores', the decline of traditional fishing and the villages it centred around accelerated. Many Skateraw fishers moved to Torry, close to Aberdeen Harbour, which offered better employment opportunities; others relocated to Cowie and Stonehaven. By 1929 only six small fishing boats remained in Skateraw employing fewer than ten people.

The decline of Skateraw was mirrored by a steady increase in the popularity of Newtonhill with business-folk from Aberdeen, who purchased former fishing cottages, initially as holiday homes but increasingly as permanent homes. The village offered fresh air, attractive surroundings and easy commuting to Aberdeen by train. The closure of Newtonhill Station in 1956 led to increasing reliance on transport by car, while the oil boom of the 1970s saw pressure for house building in the village.

Skateraw tried stubbornly to hold on to its identity and had no street names until 1968, with houses merely referred to by a number, such as 20 Skateraw (later 20 Newtonhill), but was finally forced to conform. Change inevitably continued, and by 1986 only one full-time boat remained fishing from the Elsick Shore, landing crabs and lobsters. The last twenty years have seen the demand for new housing continue to grow, a trend that looks set to continue as increasing numbers of people seek the many benefits of this attractive and healthy coastal location with its strong community spirit.

The fishing village known as Muchalls originally lay about a mile south of its current centre, beyond Doonie Point at Muchalls Shore, just south of Mill of Muchalls. It was known as the Seatoun of Muchalls, and is believed to have been situated on the high sloping ground above the shore to the north.

The earliest record of a fishertoun at this location dates from 1606 when Sir Archibald Alexander Burnett of Leys (the builder of Muchalls Castle) bought 'the lands of Muchalls, including the fishertoun, fisherlands and fisherboats' from Francis Hay, Earl of Errol and Baron of Cowie. It is, however, likely that the settlement dated from medieval times, and along with Elsick and Cowie probably formed one of the three original fishertouns of the Barony of Cowie, possibly gaining its own identity from around the 1380s when the barony was divided.

Seatoun of Muchalls is mentioned in various documents from 1606 through to *c*.1760, including the parish registers of Fetteresso. The references suggest a small but fairly stable fishing village, operating between one and four boats employing up to twenty fishermen and boys, with a maximum population of around 60 villagers.

The fishertoun did not escape its share of tragedies, and it is recorded in the parish register that on 5 February 1749 the crew of a boat from the Seatoun perished after capsizing in a storm. Although the vessel was later washed up at Skatie Shore, Cowie, superstition meant that it was not reclaimed, even being avoided for firewood for fear of incurring bad luck. On 13 December 1758 a boat's crew of six was lost when their vessel was 'overset while entering the harbour' at Muchalls.

The *Aberdeen Journal* of 8 April 1760 carried an advert for the 'roup [sale by auction] of Muchalls Estate', including the manor, milltoun, fishertoun and tenanted fisherlands. Reference was also made to a harbour or pier 'made out at a very considerable charge, for the convenience of bringing lime by sea to the tenants', although few traces remain of this structure today.

The two accidents referred to above, and the further reduction in numbers of fishermen as a result of losses to the Royal Navy press gangs who operated on shore (in addition to Royal Navy tenders which intercepted fishing boats at sea off the coast seeking recruits), led to the decline and eventual abandonment of the Seatoun of Muchalls. Some of its inhabitants moved to Stonehaven or other fishing villages to the south; others turned to different trades in the local area such as weaving, smithing or farming. Around 1818 a replacement fishing village, known as Stranathro, was established on the Estate of Muchalls and this grew steadily as a fishing and farming community (with regular cattle fairs) over the next 100 years, becoming present-day Muchalls.

While Stranathro's economy thrived, its sanitary conditions left much to be desired. A report of the mid-1800s described it as 'composed of wretched hovels, built of clay, and thatched with straw. It has no drainage,

roads ankle deep in mud and dunghills outside its front doors, these dunghills made up of fish offal and other abominations'. Such conditions had to change, and in 1856 work began to create a 'model village', forming part of the Muchalls still recognised today. This was undertaken by the land committee of Dr Milne's trustees (the then proprietor) and included 'the rebuilding of almost the whole village, the remaking of roads, introduction of water and a thorough system of drainage'. It is believed that it was around this time that the name Muchalls was adopted in preference to Stranathro (although the old name is still recalled in Stranathro Terrace in the village).

The precise derivation of the name Muchalls is not clear, but on old maps the name Montquhallis often appears with *moine* meaning a moss and *coille* referring to a wood or forest in Gaelic. An alternative derivation translates *mugach allan* as 'dark burn'. The nature of the landscape and evidence that the area was once wooded favours the first theory, while some less charitable locals have claimed the name simply means a 'mucky pond'.

The development of the model village of Muchalls appears to have been a success, and in 1896 William Paul, who lived in Stranathro Cottage, wrote positively about it in his book *Muchalls on the Kincardineshire Coast – a Health Resort*, observing: 'it is an object of interest being the first of a series of villages with which the coast is studded, to be raised from a condition quite unfit for human habitation to a state of comfort and sanitary excellence'.

This era of prosperity was in reality relatively short-lived, as in 1879 (seventeen years before Paul published his book) many of those inhabitants of the model village who earned a living from fishing were – like their neighbours in Skateraw – forced by economic circumstances and changes in the industry to seek alternative employment (and consequently much poorer accommodation) in Aberdeen or Stonehaven. By 1891 there were no more fishermen recorded as living in Stranathro, and their empty houses were quickly taken up by landward tenants, and in some cases by Aberdeen business-people keen to secure property with fresh air and sea views.

The last hundred years has seen some additional housing development take place in Muchalls, but this has been modest in comparison to that in similar villages such as Newtonhill and Portlethen. Conservation Area status and lack of drainage capacity for large-scale housing has ensured that much of the charm of the village has been retained, protecting it from overdevelopment.

Taken from Cranhill (282 ft), located to the north-east of Newtonhill and the highest point in the area, this picture dates from around 1903 and illustrates what were then the two distinct parts of the village. The original fishing community of Skateraw consisted of a group of buildings clustered around the Braehead (foreground), overlooking the bay and straggling up the hill to the smaller cluster of houses – which included the grocer's shop and public house at the top of the Skateraw Road – all of which lay on the seaward side of the railway line. Newtonhill, the 'new' part of the village, named after the croft of the same name near the main Aberdeen Road, comprised the three larger villas with dormer windows at the top right of the picture, the station, St Crispin's Croft and Newtonhill Croft, all on the landward side of the railway (see page 21). Crollshillock Farm and another small croft are visible to the left of the three villas, just below the skyline, accessed by the road that is now Park Place. Skateraw is still the traditional name used by some older residents, but generally the whole settlement is now referred to as Newtonhill.

This view shows the thatched fisher cottage nearest Braehead located immediately to the right of the top of the path up from the shore in the upper photograph.

This view of Newtonhill from the Braehead dates from *c*.1912 and shows the fishing shore with Cranhill in the background. The old Fishertoun of Elsick is thought to have been located on the lower slope of Cranhill, directly above the sea cliff and to the right of the path leading up the hill to Downies. Careful inspection of this area reveals some evidence of levelled terraces and remnants of building stone, foundations and walls. Visible in the centre is the smaller of the village's two fishing bothies, with the larger salmon fishers' bothy to its left, accessed by the original right of way across the bridge over the Elsick Burn and on to Downies. Both are now family homes. Various items of fishing paraphernalia are evident on the beach: a selection of huts for storing gear; poles and ropes for drying nets; creels; and a variety of boats. Of particular interest is the windlass at the bottom left-hand corner of the picture, used to haul fishing boats as far as possible above the high water mark. This was hard physical work which fell largely to the women of the village when the boats returned from sea. They would turn the windlass by pushing against the four poles, winding a rope attached to the boat around it and thereby hauling it up the shore.

This close-up view shows the salmon fishermen's bothy, perched above the tumbling waters of the Elsick Burn as it reaches the sea. The sea-netting of salmon was once an important element of the local fishing industry, with wild salmon previously much more prolific than they are today. Note the group of people in their Sunday best, complete with hats, who were likely to have been day trippers or holiday home owners rather than locals.

The Salmon Fishermen's Bothy, Newtonhill.

Holmes.
Silver City Series.

The Skateraw Fisherman
by Andrew Christie

Three Skateraw fishermen enjoying a 'news' on a bench on the Braehead. The photograph dates from December 1900 and is believed to show two members of the Christie family from Cairngrassie Farm to the left and right. The fisherman in the middle has not been identified.

While fermin' folk an' office folk
Are a' still fast asleep
The fishermen are aff to reap
The harvest o' the deep
Ye hear the clatter o' sea boots
Afore the break o' day
As they set off wi' baited lines
Doon the shore brae.
It disna' tak' them very lang
Wi' three men to a boat
To push them doon the shingle
An' get them a' afloat.
If there's a breeze to fill their sails
They're seen far fae the shore
The Grun' o' Crags their target
Aboot five mile or more.
The lines a' shot, they hae a smoke
Until it's time to haul
Eight hundred hooks on ilka line
It taks tae fill the scull.
By this time noo, the wives are up
They hae their work as weel
They mak' theirsels a cup o' tea
The mussels start to sheel
But when the boatie's comin' in
At the windlass they are waitin'
Wi' a muckle creel to haud the fish
That they're anticipatin'.
The wives they tak' the sculls up first
Wi the lines a' dreepin' weet
An' hae the breakfast ready
When the men come up tae eat.
When breakfast's ower, they start to gut
The fish, an' wash an' split them

An' then they're sautit in a tub
Until it's time to spit them.
The dinner noo gets underway
An' the housework a' got by
An' the lines a' on the spiltry
An' a' hung oot tae dry.
The dinner past, nae time tae sit
It's time that they were yokit
Tae spit the fish an fill the reest
An' get them a' weel smokit.
Twa hours it taks tae smoke them richt
Wi' sawdust an' wi' peat
The smoke's sae thick when ye lookin'
It nearly mak's ye greet.
The men noo start tae redd the lines
They'll hae tae bait the morn
They've hooks an' tippins to replace
Where they've broke off or worn.
The fish a' smoked, the lines a' redd
An' yet their work's nae deen
The line's tae bait, eight hundred hooks
Wi' paper in between.
They kent nae ither thing but work
An' had nae time to play
They'd slave six days in every week
An' rest the Sabbath Day.
They'd dress up in their Sunday best
An' walk up the Auld Road
Tae the service in St Ternan's
Tae give their thanks tae God.
By singin' a' the weel kent hymns
An' bowin' their heads in prayer
They were a breed o' hardy folk,
That we will see nae mair.

Some time in the 1930s a coal boat ran aground and broke up on rocks outside Newtonhill Harbour. Resourceful locals salvaged all the coal they could, and also laid claim to the ship's lifeboat, which was then repaired, repainted and renamed *Wild Rose*. For years it lay on the Newtonhill shore and visitors came from all around to pose for photos such as this one. The men in the boat have not been identified, but it is thought that they are from Aberdeen and not locals. The owner of the photograph, Arthur Wyllie, was born in Newtonhill, and is keen to trace Mary Watt or other descendants of the Watt family who stayed at No. 4 Ocean Place (now Old Mill Road) and then Rambler Cottage, Newtonhill. Anyone with any information about this local family is asked to get in touch via the publisher.

Moses Wood Jnr. hard at work repairing a creel. His father, also called Moses, was born at No. 17 Skateraw in 1886. Moses Jnr. was latterly raised in Downies with his sister Jeannie.

Catching the fish was only part of the story: having been landed and cleaned, it still had to be sold. Some cod and ling would be salted overnight and then dried in the sun (speldings) to give it a longer life, and this formed a large part of the winter diet when times were hard. Much, particularly haddock, was smoked over peat and sawdust to create the famed Finnan haddies. Selling the fish, whether fresh, salted or smoked, either entailed the womenfolk trudging round local farms and cottar houses 'cadging', or alternatively a visit to Aberdeen on Fridays. Early in the morning some fishwives would carry part of the week's catch of fish, loaded into their creels, the twelve miles from Skateraw to the market at the Green in the city (seen here). By midday their catch would generally be sold, after which they would fill their creels with provisions for the following week – or some stones to maintain their posture and balance – and trudge the twelve miles back to Skateraw.

Some Skateraw fishwives had stances at the Green close to the well at the entrance to the new market where the familiar cries of 'Caller haddocks, Finnan haddocks come and buy! Come awa' mistress, come and buy!' were frequently heard. The fishwives of the north Kincardine villages were well-known for having 'a frame strong and well knit, a comely face, a frank and hearty manner and the gift o' the gab': characteristics which were all clearly beneficial for the transportation and disposal of their fish! Life was undoubtedly hard for a Skateraw fishwife, as although the fishermen worked long, cold hours at sea, onshore the women collected the bait, baited the lines, cleaned, prepared, transported and sold the catch, looked after the house and family, and normally controlled the finances too. The coming of the railway in 1849 offered some relief from this burden as a few years later the Great North of Scotland Railway introduced special 'fishwife concession fares', which allowed the women to transport their creels to both Aberdeen and more distant centres more easily.

Looking north over Skateraw from the railway bridge to the cliffs and sea, *c*.1905. The cottages in the picture are those which flanked Skateraw Road, the main street in the village. They were built in 'but n' ben' style with a single room at each end and a door in the middle, using stones from the beach or nearby fields, with heather, broom, straw or corrugated iron employed for roofing (several of the houses in the centre of the picture were still thatched at this time). The village grew haphazardly, with houses built as they were needed or as conditions allowed, often on land that could not readily be used for agriculture. As fishing declined and the cottages were bought as summer houses or permanent residences they were improved, with slates replacing leaking thatch, dormer windows and porches added, and limewashed walls introduced.

Looking south towards Newtonhill from the cliffs on the north side of the bay, with the village's substantial pier featuring prominently. Sadly this fell into disuse and following continued storm damage was demolished in the early 1980s for safety reasons, with the remains dumped on Cranhill (although little trace of these can now be seen). Clearly visible to the right of the picture on the cliff path, above the fishermen's huts, are a row of anti-tank blocks. These three-foot cubes of reinforced concrete, with beach stones set into the top face for camouflage, were cast in-situ by local volunteers. Anti-tank blocks formed part of the Second World War coastal defences for the north-east of Scotland and were installed under the instructions of Chief Royal Engineer G. A. Mitchel in response to the German aircraft and Graf Zeppelin which had been spotted photographing the north-east coastline in great detail in 1938. It was assumed that this was in anticipation of a future beach landing invasion. The anti-tank blocks have now been removed, as have many other defence features along the coast such as pillboxes and gun emplacements. Many, however, still remain (e.g. anti-tank blocks on the clifftop at Muchalls), and are recorded in the Defence of Britain project at the Imperial War Museum.

Here lies the whale of scripture fame,
Which carried Jonah o'er the main,
He'll roam no more, make no man wrench,
He's buried deep to hide the stench.

Salmon fishing was clearly an important part of the economy of Newtonhill, as this postcard view dating from around 1909 and captioned 'Among the Salmon Fishers' shows. Salmon fishing rights belonged to the Crown or the larger estates and were let to tenants. On the east coast of Scotland the salmon fishing season lasted from early February to late August. During this time local fishermen often lived and slept in their bothy, as twelve-hour shifts were common with the men working according to the tides. Stake and bag nets, hand-knitted from cotton twine with special wooden needles, were placed in shallow coastal waters to intercept the salmon as they swam parallel to the shore in search of their home river. The fishermen rowed their cobles out to these nets twice a day to remove the fish from them. These bag nets were left in position for five days a week, being removed on Friday evenings and replaced on Monday mornings to allow the free passage of some salmon to their spawning rivers to preserve stocks. The fish were put into wooden boxes and either packed with ice and stored in an ice house, or transported to market. There is a suggestion that there may have been some form of ice house attached to the salmon fishers' bothy at Newtonhill, but this cannot be confirmed. During breaks in fishing and at the end of the season the nets were carefully looked after. This picture shows some of them strung up on wooden poles on the drying greens to dry in the wind between use. In 1913 a dead whale became entangled in the salmon nets at Newtonhill. The fishers cut it up and buried it, with the event recorded locally in the rhyme reproduced above.

The exact date of the establishment of Elsick Mill is difficult to determine, but an earlier and much smaller mill appears to have been in operation here in the late eighteenth century, and this was probably extended in the mid-nineteenth century to form the building seen here. It was constructed for grinding the oats and barley produced in the surrounding area, using the waters of the Elsick Burn as a source of power. In 1849 the railway viaduct in the background was built as part of the Stonehaven to Aberdeen railway line, and survived despite several attempts to destroy it during the Second World War when German planes flew low over the village on bombing raids. The millpond (part of which still exists) lay in the shadow of the railway viaduct and fed the various mill wheels via a series of sluices and channels. The mill continued to work through both world wars until around 1948 under Eric Muir, the last miller, after which it began to descend into ruin. Its two most recent owners have carried out extensive restoration work, converting it into a fine private residence. The former miller's house on the hill has also been restored as a house, now known as 'The Retreat'.

The Skate Raw, Newtonhill.

Holmes
Silver City Series

A *c.*1913 view looking down Skateraw, the oldest street in Newtonhill, towards the Braehead. The photographer has persuaded a number of locals to pose for his photograph. The changes which were gradually taking place in the village around this time are evidenced by the original thatched fisher cottage centre-left, flanked by two slated and whitewashed holiday or commuter homes. A pavement of sorts has been created on one side of the road, but the open spring still runs down the street.

A.3586.

"THE BAKERY," NEWTONHILL.

The bakery has always been one of the focuses of village life in Skateraw. In the 1900s it was run by Robert R. Braik, but by *c.*1910 J. S. Rogers was in charge. J. S. Walker, clothier, occupied the premises next door at the time. This picture, taken in 1936, shows the bakery when it was run by E. Milton. In its early days the bakery was particularly important to village life, as when the postman delivered the mail from Stonehaven to Skateraw it was handed to the baker who displayed it in the shop window until it was claimed, a practice which locals recall continuing until around 1912.

The Taylor family were well-known in Skateraw as they ran the general store. This photograph shows their original general merchant's store at the top of Skateraw Road with George Taylor, who ran the shop with the help of Kitty Mill, standing outside. Alongside is George's brother Jamie, who was also involved in the business but later emigrated to Washington DC. Subsequently the shop also incorporated the village post office, which was latterly run by J. & G. Taylor.

This view of the interior of George Taylor's post office and general store is believed to have been taken around 1910. Behind the counter are Geordie Taylor, his wife Nell and Lizzie Kemp. Judging by the paper chains, boxes of crackers and Christmas stockings on display the photograph was taken at Christmas time. It formed part of a calendar which is believed to have been handed out to regular customers by Geordie Taylor.

POST OFFICE, NEWTONHILL.

94474. JV.

Business was clearly good for the Taylor family in Skateraw, as in 1912 George Taylor moved his shop across the road to new enlarged premises. By this time he had diversified and was advertising as a grocer, newsagent, stationer and coal merchant, with his shop incorporating the village post office and telegraph office. Here George is see with his Ford model T delivery van. One of his brothers (there were a total of thirteen Taylor siblings), Alex, was also enjoying business success at this time, as following an accident on the railway where he had worked he established Taylor's Art Saloon at 47 Schoolhill, Aberdeen, along with a very successful travelling photographic business.

Taken in October 1922 looking down Skateraw Road from the railway line, this photograph shows George Taylor's shop on the right, along with his delivery van (on the road) and a customer's car parked in front of the shop. The open ground on the right, uphill from the shop, is the old quoiting ground where the Quoiters pub now stands. On Skateraw Road (which was somewhat in need of repair at the time!), the continuing redevelopment of the former fishermen's cottages is evidenced by the increasing number of dormer windows in view.

In 1937 George Watt moved from Dunecht to Newtonhill to establish a butcher's and poulterer's business in the premises previously occupied by the Taylors' shop. Mr Watt initially lodged in Skateraw Road with a Mrs Christie, the wife of the local baker (who subsequently moved to Torphins and opened the Sunshine Cafe). Then in November 1938 he married Nan Melrose and moved into a property called Duncot, previously owned by the Duncan family, where the Watts lived above the shop. The photograph shows Duncot with the delivery van which George Watt used to deliver orders to the surrounding farms and villages when he closed up for the day. The business operated until 1942 when George was called up for active service in the Second World War.

Until the 1930s these buildings in Sea View Terrace – together with St Crispin's and Newtonhill Crofts to the west – were the only ones which lay on the landward side of the railway, and hence made up the whole of Newtonhill (Skateraw was situated on the seaward side of the railway). The building in the foreground was originally an Episcopalian schoolhouse and replaced an earlier Episcopalian school, run from 1846 to 1855 by Effie Wishart at 18 Skateraw. In his book *The Episcopal Chapel at Muchalls*, published in 1956, John Paul Hill describes the school as 'assembling in a rented cottage perfectly ruinous', and Effie's teaching thus: 'for the last seven years a school has been taught in the village by an elderly woman, whose services have been attended with considerable benefits to the inhabitants. This arrangement however is found to be wholly insufficient . . . owing partly to the smallness and unsuitableness of the school room . . . and partly to the age and infirmities of the teacher, and her inability to impart anything beyond the simplest rudiments of Education . . . she being indeed but one of the villagers themselves.' When the second school closed it was subsequently used as a church hall until destroyed by fire in 1941. It was then replaced by the St Michael's Mission Church and an adjoining house, which again in turn was replaced by the current Newtonhill Parish Church. The other buildings remain as houses in the street now known as Elsick Place.

Station, Newtonhill — *Monday morning waiting the Train*

This early 1900s postcard shows Newtonhill Station from the southbound platform. The northbound side is thronged with people awaiting the Monday morning train to Aberdeen. Newtonhill Station opened on 1 November 1849 and closed on 11 June 1956. Attempts in the past few years to have it reopened have, to date, come to nothing. Sadly most traces of the original station have now vanished, with the exception of the signal box which still brings the occasional intercity train to a shuddering halt in the village.

This photograph was taken in the 1930s from the footbridge over the railway and shows the southbound platform and station buildings. The men standing on the platform are believed to be local bobby PC Williams, and Jim Duncan the railway porter. On Ocean Place (now called Old Mill Road), behind the station buildings, the Newton Arms pub can be seen in the middle distance, along with Milton's Newtonhill bakery on the corner, complete with the once ubiquitous Lyons Tea advert outside. To the far left some railway trucks can be seen in the goods yard sidings.

NEWTONHILL FROM THE RAILWAY BRIDGE.

A.3588.

This postcard from the late 1930s clearly illustrates Newtonhill's transition away from fisher village, with many of the former but n' ben cottages now extended and sporting dormer windows. By this time the fishing heritage was dying and Aberdeen business-folk were moving in, gradually replacing the local characters. This transition is best described in another poem by Andrew Christie, reproduced on the facing page.

Skateraw – the Village that Died

Just ten miles sooth o' Aiberdeen
A fishin' village could be seen
Perched abeen the rocky shore
Where 70 fishermen, maybe more
Each made a livin' at the sea
At the turn o' the century.
Hooever, progress marches on
The trawlers cam', the fish were gone
Nae langer could they there survive
They moved to Torry or Steenhive
Nae mair will Skateraw hear the names
O' the men wha had to leave their hames
There's Codlin', Loupie, Swak, an' Major,
Their names wad nearly fill a ledger
In winter, fan the boats cam in
The man, half frozen, weet to the skin
Each wife cam' doon tae meet her man
Wi' hauf a mutchkin in her haun
Nae sae much a celebration
But just tae start the circulation
'Jing' an' 'Auld Ondie' they stayed on
an' 'Bruxie', sometime ca'd Auld John
But time wore on, they got ower auld
An' couldna' stan the weet an' cauld
An' so the younger anes took ower
There warna' mony, three or fower.
The big boats they were a' awa'
An' sma' anes left, there were but twa
Were there, the trade tae carry on,
The *Pansy* an' *Kate Anderson*
The years wore on, their time was past
The fishin' village died at last
There were some worthies bade there still
In the place that's noo called Newtonhill
Jeck Riddell was a couthy chiel
Wha fermed the Villagelands sae weel
Jeck was aye ready fan iver bidden
Tae ca' some coals or teern a midden
Jock Craig, a big man in his day
When sober, nae a word wad say

But when he had a drink, they tell
He'd beat the dictionary a' tae hell
Then Lang Fred Moir, ill spliced thegither
Never married, lived wi' 'is mither
Rock fishin' he did quite a lot
The Braidsteen wis his fav'rit spot
At whist he played a real good hand
As quiet as ony in the land
But he wad nearly wreck the place
Gin onybody trumped his ace
Geordie Taylor at the shop
Was liked by one an' all
He sold them a' their worldly needs
Fae comic cuts tae coal
The wives he greetit wi' a smile
Nae matter whaur they came
The lairds wife or the cotter wife
He kent them a' by name
Roger had the baker's shop
Up nearby the station
The only ane for miles aroon
A wonderful location
The smells that was come waftin' oot
When he wad start tae bake
The God's Ambrosia can't compare
Wi' Roger's baps an' cake
George Lamb lived by the joiner's shop
An' dearly loved a drappie
In the pub he'd book a corner seat
An' there he'd stay quite happy
Waddy lived beyond the pub
But he just moved there lately
He used to live in number six
Wi' sister Jean sae stately
His sayins werna' very bricht
In fact, some were just plain silly
'My wireless says it's rain today,
fit diz yours say, Willie?'
Then richt across the railway line
The signal box was there

Nae mony trains rin past there noo
In these days there were mair
Three signalmen, a' sonsy chiels
Each worked eight hours a day
Will Christie an' Jeck Duncan
The third was Jimmy Rae.
A bricht an' spotless signal box
Was the fruits o' their endeavours
For they took pride in a weel scrubbed
   fleer
An' burnished signal levers
Davie Kemp, a kindly chiel
At souterin nane could beat
He lived up in the Souters Road
It's noo St Crispin's Street
Davie was a first class hand
At playin' at the quoits
An mony a game the team wad play
In the lang licht summer nichts
The fisher hooses, up for sale
Didna' lang bide teem
But were bocht by business folk wha wad
Commute fae Aiberdeen
There were a lot o' weel kent folks
Cam' oot there just for pleasure
They'd sweem aboot doon I' the shore
or just relax at leisure
There was Strachan, number twenty
   three
He worked for E and M
An' Whyte, aye smokin' a cigar
A painter on his ain
John Fenton O' the Northern Ice
An' Gilchrist had a bar
McKenzie, a solicitor
Look doon upon the shore
Robertson the tinsmith
Lived there for mony a day
He bocht the *Mary Watson*
Tae sail aroon the bay

Pat Grant, he was anither
Made's money cuttin' hair
He ca'd his hoose 'Pitullie'
'cos his wife she cam' fae there
Jeanie Hendry lived there too
She was a dancin' teacher
An' doon fae her was Maister Yuill
A Plymouth Brethren preacher
They had a fitba' team that won
The Panmure cup ae year
At their hame games the local folk
Would a' turn oot tae cheer
After the game, the weary players
A' the twenty twa
Had tea, prepared by Agg an' Liz
Doon I' the Village Hall
But that's a' deen awa' wi' noo
It's nae the same ava'
There's only twa-three natives left
The rest's a' moved awa'
It really is amazin'
The way the place has spread
There's hooses noo fae Bettridge
Richt roon tae Millers ned
A braw new school's been biggit
Not far fae the station
Wi' a' the new equipment
For the bairns education
Scores of new houses have been built
Semis and self contained
But the residential status
The planners have maintained
Nae factories belchin' smoke are here
The air is fresh and clean
There's nae a village like it
Tween Steenhive and Aiberdeen
When you see the braw new hooses
Yer herts wi' pride instill
You ane and a' can proudly say
I came fae Newtonhill

ELSICK NEWTONHILL

Elsick House is an impressive mansion which lies about a mile to the north-west of Newtonhill. It has been the home of the lairds of the Elsick Estate, the Bannerman family, almost continuously since around 1382. The oldest part of the house may have medieval origins but the majority of the structure is more recent, having been rebuilt after a serious fire in 1754. In 1756 the house and lands were sold out of Bannerman family ownership by Sir Alexander Bannerman (4th baronet), but were repurchased by the 9th baronet in 1851 and have passed through the female line to the Carnegie Earls of Southesk. The current owner, the Duke of Fife, is the present chief of the Carnegies.

This photograph was taken on 24 September 1937 in the grounds of Elsick House on the occasion of the master of Carnegie's eighth birthday party. He is standing on the far right of the picture, wearing a kilt and sporran. Immediately to his left are two notable guests at the party, the Princesses Elizabeth and Margaret Rose.

Muchalls from the West

This view of Muchalls looking north-east from the fields to the south of the village dates from around 1915 and shows the rear of the former Marine Hotel (demolished 2004) on the right. The residential property in the centre of the picture is called Viewfield (see page 37), while on the skyline to the left is the row of coastguard cottages in Marine Terrace (see page 34). The coastguard station comprised seven individual houses, plus the chief coastguard's house and an equipment shed.

The predecessor of the Marine Hotel was built in 1856 and was called the Muchalls Inn. By the 1890s it was known as the Muchalls Hotel, had six bedrooms and was contributing significantly to the popularity of Muchalls as a developing health resort and summer Mecca for tourists. In 1896 a contemporary description of the village boasted that, 'for pure and bracing air, and its varied scenery, Muchalls stands unrivalled'. Of the Muchalls Hotel, the same guide said: 'It is a pretty and cheerful sight, suggestive of the old and new order of things, to observe a handsome four-in-hand coach with its team of bays or dapple greys, hired for the day by a merry party, discharging its passengers at the door, and scattered about and leaning against every convenient support, bicycles of the most recent pattern vying with each other in the elegance of their appointments and beauty of finish'. In 1900 sixteen further bedrooms were added to the hotel to upgrade it to the status of 'station hotel', at which point it became known as the Marine Hotel. This picture shows the size of the extended hotel, with a number of guests enjoying the pleasures of the croquet lawn.

This carefully posed view dates from about 1915. A publicity brochure for the hotel from around this time noted its telephone number as Newtonhill 2 and boasted that it 'offered every amenity associated with a modern hotel – electric light, hot and cold water in all bedrooms, adequate bathroom accommodation and garage facilities'. Leisure facilities on offer included a 9-hole golf course, hard tennis courts, putting green and croquet lawn. The cuisine was given special mention with all dairy produce supplied from Lord Carnegie of Elsick's famous 'Model Dairy Farm' (which could be visited by appointment), vegetables from the hotel garden, and salmon 'fresh from the sea at Muchalls', all prepared in the kitchens on the 'latest type of ESSE Heat Storage Cooker'. The French-sounding ESSE name reflected the fashion at that time for continental-style stoves, although this brand actually hailed from an iron foundry in Bonnybridge. ESSE cookers came highly recommended, with Florence Nightingale among those who were passionate about them, refusing to use any other at her hospital in Balaclava. Later, famous British explorers Shackleton and Scott, whose lives often depended upon the performance of their equipment during expeditions to some of the world's most inhospitable places, relied on an ESSE to provide hot food and warmth to their team. Indulging in the luxury accommodation offered by the Marine Hotel cost three to five guineas per person per week, all-inclusive. Sadly in recent years the hotel closed and fell steadily into disrepair. A fire badly damaged the building in 2002 and it was demolished in 2004, due shortly to be replaced by new 'executive' housing.

This photograph shows team- and staff-members of Aberdeen Football Club with some locals and the manager and trainer of Chelsea FC outside the Marine Hotel at Muchalls, where Chelsea were staying for a challenge match with Aberdeen at Pittodrie stadium on 26 September 1955. The teams were English and Scottish league champions at the time. A crowd of 20,000 saw the Dons beat Chelsea 4–3, with a hat-trick from Paddy Buckley and Bobby Wishart adding a fourth. Ted Drake, the Chelsea manager, said after the match: 'I should think that, at the moment, Aberdeen are without doubt the best side in Scotland'. The owners of the hotel at that time, Mr and Mrs Walker, are standing far left and seated front row, third from left, with Ted Drake, the Chelsea manager, seated at the far left of the front row. The teams for the match were as follows:

Aberdeen: Martin, Paterson, Mitchell, Wilson, Clunie, Glenn, Leggat, Yorston, Buckley, Wishart, Hather.

Chelsea: Robertson, Harris, Willemse, Armstrong, Wicks, Saunders, Parsons, McNichol, Bentley, Smith, Kitchener.

This photograph shows, left to right: the Chelsea trainer (name unknown); Jimmy Herd (Muchalls); Bob Wallace (Muchalls); and Ted Drake, the Chelsea manager, teeing off from the first hole of Muchalls golf course during their stay at the Marine Hotel for the challenge football match. The course was instituted in 1908 and officially opened in May 1909 by George Walker of Portlethen. Its nine holes covered some 30 acres between the main Aberdeen road and the railway line, and South Station Road and the Burn of Muchalls. The course was laid out by the Aberdeen Educational Trust and when it opened visitors were charged a shilling per day, four shillings per week or ten shillings per month to use it. The course was given up on 23 January 1968.

Mill of Muchalls (now called East Muchalls Farm) seen looking west towards the railway viaduct. Like Elsick Mill, this was another local mill used for grinding oats and barley, in this case driven by water from the Burn of Muchalls (right). The waterwheel is just visible on the left-hand side of the building. From here the burn flows eastwards for a short distance, forming a tranquil pool before entering the sea via a waterfall. This pool was where the scene of Ophelia's drowning was shot in the film *Hamlet*, starring Mel Gibson and directed by Franco Zeffirelli. Much of the filming was carried out near Stonehaven at Dunnottar Castle, and parts of a mock castle were also erected in this area at Mill of Muchalls for filming the nighttime scenes. The picture also shows two fine haystacks, a very rare sight these days.

Dating from *c*.1900, this picture shows the salmon fishers' bothy which was located on the clifftop to the north of Mill of Muchalls, the remains of which are still visible today among the undergrowth. Note the racks for drying the salmon nets, the herring hake to the right of the bothy door for drying fish, and the fine salmon held by the fisherman, perhaps destined for the Marine Hotel.

Of the many caves along the coast, several have interesting histories. One, near Mill of Muchalls, was home to a hardy character called Adam Middleton (better known as 'Nippie'), who lived there in the early 1900s. His lifestyle must have been harsh, with only an old sack over the cave mouth to keep out the sharp winds from the sea. Nippie survived, by all accounts, on a diet of shellfish, plus rabbits left on a rock near his cave by gamekeepers on the local estate. He earned pocket money by doing odd jobs for local farmers, and was also occasionally paid for painting the sleepers on the railway. During the summer he lived in his rocky abode but in the winter he apparently moved in with his sister, who had a house in Dunnottar Woods near Stonehaven. The nickname Nippie is widely believed to come from his fondness for a nip of whisky, but it has also been claimed that it derived from his time as a drummer in the Boer War, when his fleetness of foot was put to good use as a foot messenger at times when horse messengers were unable to get through. Both explanations seen plausible. Sadly, Nippie's undoubted love of a dram led to his untimely death in 1910, when he was struck and killed by a train, in the dark, while walking back to his cave along the railway line after visiting the Marine Hotel in Muchalls. After his death, local people filled in part of the cave to prevent anyone else living there, and his memory lives on in local folklore today.

Smuggling was a serious problem all along the north-east coast in the eighteenth and nineteenth centuries as the many coves, caves and rocky inlets proved difficult to police and hence ideal for the illicit trade in gin, rum, tobacco, tea and silk from overseas, all of which were brought ashore clandestinely to avoid paying heavy excise duties. As many of the boats, including fishing vessels, were small, open and hard to identify, the government passed a law whereby the owner's name and home port had to be painted on all boats. The establishment of what is now HM Coastguard dates from 1815, when several existing bodies, most of which had originally been formed to combat smuggling, were combined, and until 1831 coastguards remained under the control of HM Customs and Excise. Combating smuggling, rather than rescuing sailors, remained the principal duty of coastguards until the late 1800s. The picture below shows the Muchalls coastguard station houses, which were built around 1830.

Albert Brokenshire, seen here wearing his naval medals, served with the coastguard service in Muchalls from around 1922 to 1925, and this picture was taken on the green adjacent to the coastguard houses. Two interesting features on the coastguard station building are the crown and anchor motifs on the drainpipes (denoting Admiralty ownership), and a shared internal corridor on the landward side of the building, facing on to Marine Terrace. The back doors of the seven houses originally opened into this corridor which allowed all the coastguards to be roused in case of an emergency without the need to run from house to house outside. In 1926 the Admiralty gave up the lease on the cottages, and in 1927 Mr A. Barclay Walker of Stranathro Cottage purchased all the houses and land for the sum of £1,000. They now form five houses and the internal corridor has been divided up between the properties.

Dating from *c.*1910, this picture shows the officer and crew of Muchalls coastguards with unit 218 of the Board of Trade Rocket Life Saving Apparatus (LSA) outside its storage shed in Muchalls. The building still survives as a garage for a private house. HM Coastguard trained local volunteers – many of which came from nearby fishing communities, and all of whom had seen service at sea – to use the rocket-propelled life-saving apparatus for inshore rescues. The equipment was kept in a cart which was drawn to the scene of a stricken vessel either by hand or by horse, then rockets would be fired, dragging rescue lines to survivors on the vessel, who would then be hauled ashore by breeches buoy. The Muchalls LSA unit was formed in 1870, and in 1887 consisted of some 25 volunteers who assisted the established coastguards in many inshore rescues over the years. There were regular inspections of the unit and it won many awards for performance and bravery, including best unit in Britain. In 1841 Richard Brunton was the chief coastguard officer at Muchalls. His son, Richard Henry Brunton (1841–1901), became an engineer and achieved fame in 1868 when he went to Japan as chief engineer to the Japanese government's lighthouse department, supervising a scheme for the installation of lighthouses along the entire coastline of Japan. In 1923 the Muchalls coastguard came under the control of the Aberdeen division.

These two views of Muchalls village are believed to date from around 1920. Seaview Terrace was the original 'front row' of the three rows of cottages created for the model village of Stranathro around 1818. It is now known as Stranathro Terrace, with the original middle and back rows forming the two sides of modern Monduff Road.

Seaview Terrace, Muchalls

In Muchalls Village

The houses at 2, 4 and 6 Dunnyfell Road. Number 4, the middle cottage in the terrace (with a pram parked outside) was the residence of the estate factor of the Aberdeen Endowments Trust which owned much of the land around Muchalls. The street derives its name from the large natural arch-shaped rock of the same name which lies on the coast to the south of the village, below Craigness.

Cliff Cottage is believed to have been built in the early 1900s by John Milne, an architect from Aberdeen. It was known as Kariba for a short period in the 1960s before reverting back to its original name.

This fine villa was built in 1837 at a cost of £400. In 1891 it was known as Rockville, then it became Viewfield in 1919/20, before being renamed Greenacres in 1950.

In the nineteenth century a typical fisher croft consisted of a two-room house with packed earth floors, sometimes sprinkled with sand or spread with old sails to reduce the dust. As work such as mending nets and preparing and baiting lines was often done indoors in bad weather, floors needed cleaning regularly. The rooms generally had only one small window, frequently without glass and instead protected by a wooden shutter. Furnishings were sparse with a table and chairs, kist or chest of drawers, and a large open peat fire which was used to cook on, smoke fish, and warm the house. The interior was consequently very smoky and walls were whitewashed to maximise light. The other room was the only bedroom and also doubled as the 'best room, ben the hoose' with its box bed hidden behind wooden shutters and the ornaments and crockery on display, as seen here, for the benefit of visitors. Above the two rooms was a loft used for drying nets and storing lines, oars etc., with most houses keeping a cat to protect the nets from damage from mice. As more of Muchalls' houses became summer holiday homes or were sold to commuters, needs changed, proper floors were installed and loft spaces were converted to living accommodation.

Muchalls' original post office was located near St Ternan's Church, situated on the main road along which the mail coaches travelled. When this postcard was produced c.1906 William Watt was the proprietor, his shop advertising the ubiquitous Fry's chocolate in the window. By the late 1920s the former post office premises were in the hands of W. G. Simpson, who traded as a tea, wine and spirit merchant, fruiterer and confectioner. From 1991 the post office in Muchalls was operated by Rosie Lang from her cottage in Marine Terrace, but sadly it finally closed its doors on 24 January 2005.

Jane McQueen and her daughter 'howkin' tatties' in the garden of Strathbarrel Cottage. Jane Sr. was believed to have been in her seventies at this time. Note the wooden-wheeled barrow in the background.

This photograph of Strathbarrel Cottage was printed privately in postcard form, complete with a 'Christmas Greeting' message so that it could be used as a Christmas card. Standing outside the cottage are Dugald and Jane McQueen and their daughter Jane.

In April 1902 a public meeting was held to decide what form the local Coronation Day celebrations should take. Over £30 was raised in subscriptions and it was decided that the families of Cairnhill, Muchalls and Newtonhill should attend a picnic followed by a bonfire and fireworks on 26 June. Edward VII's Coronation, due to take place on 24 June, was, however, postponed for six weeks due to the monarch having to undergo an emergency appendix operation. The scheduled local celebrations were also postponed, but to avoid disappointing local children a picnic was held for them on the same afternoon in the village hall and grounds of the Marine Hotel. Three decorated horses and carts were supplied by Messrs Cushnie of Blackbutts, Glegg of Elrick and Philip of Pityot, all decorated by Mr Quirie, the gardener at Muchalls Castle. Mr Philip brought the children from the school to the hotel, where they were photographed by Messrs Taylor, Schoolhill, Aberdeen, as seen here. Various races and games were laid on, along with football, with prizes donated by the public. A dance was held in the village hall in the evening. The Coronation finally took place on 9 August and the planned local celebrations went ahead the same day, as described by the *Stonehaven Journal* of 14 August 1902: 'Favoured with lovely weather the celebrations were a decided success in Newtonhill/Muchalls district. The proceedings began at 2 p.m. when a Royal Salute was fired by the Coastguards men. Sports and games were entered into most heartily, by both adults and juveniles, and the Committee provided prizes liberally. Dancing was enjoyed as long as light allowed. Tea and lemonade were supplied to more than 600 people on the picnic field. At 10 p.m. the bonfire was lit and an elaborate display of fireworks, the gift of Lady Robertson, Muchalls Castle, was then begun. In addition to the treat and medals presented each child of school age was presented with a savings bank book with 1/- put to their account. The balance of subscriptions left (30/-) is to be divided between Bridge of Muchalls and Cairnhill schools to extend their libraries.'

Muchalls' Episcopal congregation can be traced continuously from the seventeenth century. The original Muchalls chapel was constructed in 1624 by the Burnetts of Crathes as part of Muchalls Castle. It was, however, razed to the ground in 1746 on the orders of the Duke of Cumberland on his way to Culloden. In 1748 a temporary dry stone chapel was erected a few hundred yards away across a field to the north of the castle, followed by a replacement stob-thatched building in 1770. A third, tiled chapel followed in 1795. The still extant building shown above was commenced in 1831, initially a humble structure funded largely by contributions from the populations of Skateraw and Stranathro. In 1847 the church received an old ship's bell from Cowie line fishers who had fished it up from the bottom of the sea, and at the time the bell-ringer was paid the princely sum of £1 per annum. The connection of the chapel with St Ternan, a Celtic missionary who preached on the braes at Findon in the fifth century, seems to date from around the 1860s. In 1865 the apse and chancel were added to the church and in 1870 the nave was enlarged to accommodate the increasing congregation. Weddings were conducted at the church, but burials took place at the kirkyard of St Mary of the Storms at Cowie, meaning that mourners had to carry coffins on poles the five miles along the narrow clifftop paths.

Following the destruction of his church in 1746, the then minister of Muchalls, Revd John Troup, was forced to resort to using any available accommodation to preach to his followers from. Further difficulty was caused by the ban that forbade Episcopalian clerics from preaching to more than four people at any one time, introduced because of the church's support for the Jacobite cause. Despite these hindrances, he and other clergy began to assemble in larger groups, either in houses or secluded places in the open air. A publication dating from the late 1890s recalls that in 1748 'One Saturday night [Revd Troup] sent word round the villages of Skateraw and the Seatoun [of Muchalls] that he would, on the following morning, conduct a service at a place named the Goudie, a large rock situated a little to the north of the Seatoun. At the appointed time the men from Skateraw came round in their boats, but the service had scarcely commenced when the watchman, who had been placed on the top of the cliff to give warning in case of danger, came and told Revd Troup that Cumberland's redcoats were coming, someone having informed them that a service was to be held at that place. The Seatoun villagers hurriedly made tracks to their houses while the Skateraw men went hurry-scurrying home in their boats.' As a result, Revd Troup, along with Revd Greig of Stonehaven and Revd Petrie of Drumlithie, who were also found guilty of similar breaches of both these and other even more severe penal laws, were 'during the winter of 1748–49 confined for the space of six months in the Tolbooth of Stonehaven'. It is claimed that Revd Troup carried bagpipes with him on the way to jail and played the Jacobite air of *O'er the Water to Charlie*. Despite their incarceration the men continued to minister to their followers, who received divine service from the window of their communal cell. It is alleged that Revd Troup also performed numerous baptisms for the wives of fishermen from Skateraw, who trudged along the foreshore at Stonehaven with their babies concealed in their creels and clambered over the rocks to present them at the cell window at the rear of the Tolbooth. After their release, all three clergymen returned to their homes and continued to preach to their followers without further hindrance. This painting, entitled 'Baptism from the Jail at Stonehaven', is by Newcastle artist George Washington Brownlow, who lived in Muchalls for three years. It dates from 1865 and is arguably his most famous work. The models for the painting were Christies, Woods and Massons from Skateraw, all descendants of the original protagonists. High quality copies of this painting, sold to raise funds for St Ternan's Episcopal Church, can be obtained from George Masson of St Ternan's. For more details please contact George on +44 (0)1224 733583.

Muchalls Castle is an L-shaped building constructed on the foundations of an ancient Fraser fortress. It was begun in 1619 by Sir Archibald Alexander Burnett of Leys and was finished by his son, Sir Thomas Burnett, in 1627. The castle is classed as one of the baronial antiquities of Scotland, and unlike many Scottish castles and mansions has been in continuous occupation for four centuries. Internally it has fine Renaissance-style decoration, something which was becoming popular in Scotland at the time of its construction. Perhaps the castle's most famous assets are its ornate plaster ceilings, dating from around 1624 and reputed to be among the finest in Scotland. The best-known of these is that in the great hall on the first floor of the main block. The delicate white stucco is similar to work found in Glamis, Craigievar, Pinkie near Musselburgh and Winton near Tranent, but is considered superior to them all. It includes 'six coats of arms of the Burnett and allied families, fully tinctured, four medallions depicting the heads of Roman emperors, classical heroes and Old Testament characters, and three knops with hooks for hanging lamps, all joined with a pattern of straight and curved ribs bearing floral designs in relief.'

Vying with the ceiling for attention in the great hall is an enormous ornamented fireplace surmounted by the royal coat of arms, with Scottish quartering, and flanked by four Egyptian figures which were fashionable at the time the fireplace was made. The work on both the ceilings and the fireplace appears to be that of craftsmen imported specially from London. Muchalls Castle also boasts many other interesting features including a hidden staircase, a wishing well in the courtyard and a handsome canopied bed, reputedly slept in for nine nights by James Stuart, the Jacobite Old Pretender. This bed is located in the bedroom which clearly belonged to the laird, as the room also features a listening device or 'laird's lug': an aperture set into the wall running from the bedroom to the fireplace in the great hall which allowed the master of the house to monitor what was being said, even when he had 'withdrawn'!

The Gin Shore lies to the east of the old Seatoun of Muchalls, and although clearly used for fishing purposes, as this picture shows, its very name conjures up images of smuggling activities carried out in the dead of night at this rocky cove. The shore also has links with Muchalls Castle as it was reputedly the destination of the now-lost underground passage which led from the castle wine cellars, and which was allegedly used for smuggling. This secret underground passage is also the reason that Muchalls Castle supposedly has its own ghost, the 'Green Lady'. According to local legend the daughter of one of the lairds was involved in a romantic tryst with a smuggler on a boat that

plied to and from the Continent. One stormy evening, on seeing her lover's vessel approaching and in defiance of her father, she raced down the secret passageway to greet him as he rowed into the sea cave on the Gin Shore. Tragically, she slipped and tumbled into the stormy waters, was washed out to sea and drowned by the strong currents, with her body discovered nearby the next day. The ghost of the lady, dressed in green (or sometimes yellow) has been sighted in the castle on numerous occasions. Famously, in 1906, a gentleman guest, on his way down to dinner, glimpsed a young girl in a long dress in front of a mirror in one of the bedrooms making the final preparations to her hair. In the dining room he informed his hosts that he thought 'the other lady' would be down for dinner shortly, only to be told he was the only guest that night. While it was commonly believed that this passage linked the cave and the castle, no evidence exists to prove the fact. Stories abound of a piper entering the cave, playing his pipes, never to return. Local rumour has it that the passageway was blocked during the construction of the railway, or that it was sealed up in the 1890s by Lord Robertson, Lord Justice General of Scotland, who was the then tenant of Muchalls Castle and was offended by tales of such smuggling activities on his own doorstep. In 1896 the *Aberdeen Free Press* reported two men setting off to explore the cave and finding two large chambers, linked by a long, narrow tunnel 'for 100 ft little more than 3 ft wide and in one or two places only 16 in, but in some 30 to 40 ft high'. The final chamber was described as '70 ft long, 10 ft wide and 11 ft high with a floor of beach gravel sand, perfect pure and uniform, quite dry from end to end, the tide at high water does not come within several feet of the entrance'. Whilst this may have been a perfect smugglers' cave, there was no sign of a continuing passage.

This fine 1890s photograph shows a group dressed in their best clothes on the shore at the Grim Haven, Muchalls. The gentleman in the centre is Dugald McQueen, railway worker, of Strathbarrel Cottage, seen with his wife Jane seated two places to his left. The picture is thought to show either a works outing or a gathering of extended family members.

In August 1974, at its first attempt, Muchalls won Best Kept Village in the North of Scotland in a contest organised by Britain in Bloom, beating 35 other entries in the region. This photograph shows the wrought iron sign being unveiled at the entrance to the village at the top of Dunnyfell Road by Mr Lester Borley, chief executive of the Scottish Tourist Board. To the left of Mr Borley is Arthur Dunwood, vice-chairman of Muchalls Village Association.

Muchalls won Best Kept Village in the North of Scotland for the second year in succession in August 1975. This photograph shows the sign being formally handed over (it did not need to be moved on this occasion!) by Councillor Ellen Williamson (second left) of Aberdeen, a member of the Scottish Tourist Board. Chairman of the Muchalls Village Association, Dr Stephen George, is in the foreground on the right. Other proud residents of Muchalls in the picture include Margaret Reid, Miss Geddes, Dr Cummins, Mrs Walshaw, Helen Fraser, Mrs Mekie, Mrs Roberston and Mrs Reid.

Muchalls Station opened on 1 November 1849 and this photograph shows the aftermath of an accident that occurred on 21 September 1897. This took place at 2.27 a.m. (the time the station clock stopped at), and thankfully there was no loss of life as the station was unattended at the time, although serious damage amounting to several thousand pounds was done to its fabric. The 11.20 p.m. Caledonian goods train from Perth to Aberdeen, consisting of between 35 and 40 wagons, encountered a problem about a mile south of Muchalls, due it is believed to a quantity of timber with which one of the wagons was laden having 'fallen and [got] among the wheels', throwing the wagon off the rails. The length of the train and the fact that the wagon in question was near the rear meant the engine driver remained unaware of the problem until reaching the station. In the meantime the derailed wagon derailed several other trucks and wagons, and havoc ensued when the train arrived at the station, still travelling at high speed. The front of the signal box was destroyed, the overhead bridge was torn down, and the west platform was seriously damaged. Two or three wagons mounted the platform, only stopping 30 yards short of the stationmaster's house where he and his family were sleeping. The eight wagons and trucks that had left the rails were completely destroyed, as were their contents, which were described in the press as follows. 'In the wreckage of one van were discovered the carcasses of four calves which had evidently been killed outright, for some of them bore traces of severe injuries. A considerable portion of the west platform was littered with thousands of spools of woollen yarn – a consignment to some of the local factories. Several large cases of tins of paint lay battered and smashed. Quite an army of hams was strewn about and cases of clothing, collars, waterproof garments, travelling bags, and dressing cases had been broken and their contents scattered about. It were impossible almost to describe the parts of the piles of debris. Boxes of bottles of ink, cases full of clocks – reduced to hopeless wrecks – barrels and tins of paraffin – some smashed and others leaking – grosses of packages of starch, scores of bird cages and numerous wheels and buffers of wagons all bore evidence to the damage done.' Despite the severity of the accident, by 10 o'clock next morning the southbound line had been cleared, and by the evening traffic was running as usual. Clearly no detailed health and safety inquiries hindered the running of the railways in those days!